Basketball Fundamentals

by Sidney Goldstein

author of **The Basketball Coach's Bible**

and **The Basketball Player's Bible**

GOLDEN AURA PUBLISHING

The Nitty-Gritty Basketball Series

Basketball Fundamentals

by Sidney Goldstein

Published by:

GOLDEN AURA PUBLISHING

Post Office Box 41012

Philadelphia, PA 19127 U.S.A.

Second Edition Copyright © 1999 by Sidney Goldstein

Printed in the U.S.A.

Goldstein, Sidney

Basketball Fundamentals

Sidney Goldstein.--Second Edition, 1999

Basketball-Coaching

ISBN 1-884357-35-0

Softcover

Contents

Introduction

Over many years of coaching, planning, and studying, I found ways to teach each and every skill even to the most unskilled player. This scheme of learning did not come from any book. I tried things in practice. I modified them till they worked. Even players who could not simultaneously chew bubble gum and walk learned the skills. This booklet, part of **The Basketball Coach's Bible**, is one result of this effort. I believe you too can benefit from my work.

Who Can Use This Information

This booklet is the perfect tool for anybody who wants to coach, teach, and/or learn basketball:

- A parent who wants to teach his or her child
- A player who wants to understand the game better
- A little league or recreation league coach
- A high school or junior high school coach
- A college coach, a professional coach
- A women's or a men's coach

This booklet contains material from **The Basketball Coach's Bible** and **The Basketball Player's Bible**. Chapter 1 discusses the meaning and importance of fundamentals. Chapter 2 describes the court, the importance of several areas, and defines commonly used basketball terms. Chapter 3 presents the fundamentals in a graphical flow chart, while Chapter 4 presents fundamentals in a detailed outline. Study these short chapters to obtain an overall view of the game. Chapter 5 discusses the outline in detail. Because of the many references in chapters 1-5 to lessons in **The Basketball Coach's Bible**, a table of lessons from that book follows. The next chapter, entitled Principles of Learning, comes from **The Basketball Player's Bible**. It explains keys to learning each fundamental and gives many counterproductive ideas. Again, a table of lessons from **The Basketball Player's Bible** follows because of the many references.

The references to lessons are not needed to understand this material. However, they are helpful to those who want more detail and/or plan to study the larger books.

Golden Aura's Nitty-Gritty Basketball Series
by Sidney Goldstein

See the description in the back of this book.

The Basketball Coach's Bible

The Basketball Player's Bible

The Basketball Shooting Guide

The Basketball Scoring Guide

The Basketball Dribbling Guide

The Basketball Defense Guide

The Basketball Pass Cut Catch Guide

Basketball Fundamentals

Planning Basketball Practice

Videos for the Guides soon available

HOW TO CONTACT THE AUTHOR

The author seeks your comments about this book. Sidney Goldstein is available for consultation and clinics with coaches and players. Contact him at:

Golden Aura Publishing
PO Box 41012
Philadelphia, PA 19127
215 438-4459

Chapter One

1

A Philosophy of Fundamentals

Every coach agrees that the fundamentals of basketball are important. How does this translate to what we, coaches, do every day in practice? Are we just giving them lip service or do we really believe in fundamentals? Let's examine some facts:

1. The pros' foul shot percentage has always been between 63% and 68%. Why is it so low? The pros are the best players, and they surely have time to practice. What's the problem? The answer–shooting technique.

Shooting 100 foul shots does not improve your shooting technique. Shooting technique is a fundamental that both 7th graders and the pros need to practice regularly. If coaches emphasized technique, foul shooting percentages would go up 10-15%.

2. After reading many books, attending many clinics and watching many high school and college practices, I find little time spent on fundamentals. Even when they are addressed, the methods and explanations usually lack detail, completeness, and effectiveness.

3. I also perceive a widely held attitude by coaches, men's coaches in particular, that fundamentals are for little kids, little girls. These folks should calculate their team's foul shooting percentage. They should also count the number of good dribblers on their team. These numbers won't add up to nearly the number of players on the team.

4. In clinic after clinic and book after book, I find tons of info about offensive plays. I'm sure there are many entire books devoted to this topic. What's the problem? Your team's offense needs to react to the other team's defense. This involves not only adjusting to each opponent but also adjusting to each play of the game. You can't teach these adjustments by just practicing predesigned plays! Teaching the fundamentals of both individual and team offense is the only way to do it. Emphasis needs to be shifted away from plays to the fundamentals.

5. Many coaches at the high school (including myself initially) and lower levels of play think that zone defense is easier to teach than person-to-person defense. However, players in a zone must know how to cover players one-on-one in every situation, as well as how to shift properly in the zone. Thus, zones are more difficult if you look at the fundamentals involved.

If the fundamentals of basketball are like the fundamentals of physics, house building, or any thing else, then they are the building blocks for learning and doing. Skipping them at any level of play, from 7th graders to the pros, leads to problems: if you were a house builder the building would fall down. In basketball skipping these steps leads to a vacuum of information on the fundamentals and second rate training methods. Can you imagine a builder not bothering to make a strong solid foundation because the building style is so sophisticated? Yet coaches routinely ignore laying a strong foundation in favor of developing fancy "architecture."

The fundamentals are more than the building blocks. You can combine the individual and team basics to perform any skill or move or play. Slightly altering the lessons in this book can produce more configurations than you ever imagined. An example: after I spent months teaching one-on-one defense, my 10th grade players learned a 2-1-2 shifting zone in 5 minutes–actually during a double time-out in a game. Anybody can do this if he or she understands the power and significance of the fundamentals.

Another misconception about fundamentals is that they are easy to learn. This is hardly the case. They are very difficult to learn, practice, apply, and even recognize. Seventh graders will not be able to perform adequately half the things in this book. Most pros can do better, but not by as much as you think.

Many folks may have another misconception about how skillfulness relates to a player's basketball ability. They think that basketball prowess goes hand-in-hand with skill; not entirely so. This may be a surprising statement from a person who is writing about the need to emphasize fundamentals. Here is one example: how would Magic Johnson, Wilt Chamberlain, or Michael Jordan do if he were a foot shorter? Would we even know their names today if this were true? This book teaches fundamentals, not how to make great players. If you want to turn out great players, then you need to also work on genetics, speed, and strength.

This is a book of fundamentals. It is a step back to the basics and a step forward to improved training methods. It is a place to start and to return again and again. I have tried to explain the fundamentals without skipping steps for coaches at all levels. All lessons in this book can and should be modified and combined to suit your own purposes. No matter what you do, the fundamentals do not change. You will reap great reward by recognizing, practicing, and applying them to your situation.

Chapter Two

The Court

2

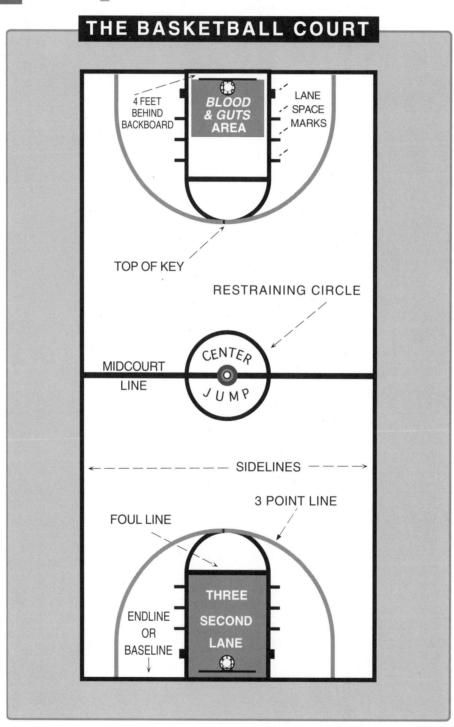

THE BASKETBALL COURT

4 FEET BEHIND BACKBOARD

BLOOD & GUTS AREA

LANE SPACE MARKS

TOP OF KEY

RESTRAINING CIRCLE

CENTER JUMP

MIDCOURT LINE

SIDELINES

3 POINT LINE

FOUL LINE

ENDLINE OR BASELINE

THREE SECOND LANE

The Court

If the court were real estate worth $1000, the area around the basket would be worth $999.99. I call this the ***blood and guts area***. Games are won and lost here. However, simply stating that this is the most important area on the court is inadequate. You need to practice and teach every lesson with this focus.

Most coaches are not aware that the court extends four feet behind the backboard. Great rebounders devastate opponents moving to the ball from this area. You need to teach offensive rebounders to use this area to their advantage. Defensive players must learn how to box out players rebounding from this direction. (Section 11–rebounding, 12.4-12.6–defense)

The Lines

All lines on the court are two inches thick. The endlines (or baselines) and sidelines border the court. The center restraining circle is twelve feet in diameter. The three second lane is bounded by the foul line on one end and the baseline on the other. The midcourt line divides the court in half. This information is hardly surprising to most people. If you step on a line you are **out** if it is an out-of-bounds line or the midcourt line. You are **in,** if it is any other line. In either case, out or in, the lines can work against you. Players must watch where they step.

The three point line, if your court has any, is a semicircle about 20 feet (more for the pros) from the basket. Since the basket is 4-6 feet from the endline, the three point line straightens out about 5 feet from the endline.

The top of the key is a point that intersects the three point line straight away from the basket. I don't think there are any rules concerning the top of the key now. In the distant past there may have been. The semicircle at the court end of the lane also has no function now. It was part of another restraining circle when jump balls were held near the tie up position. Now teams alternate possessions after a tie up in most leagues.

The foul line or free throw line is 19 feet from the baseline and 13 feet from the front rim of the basket. The basket itself is 18 inches in diameter and is 6 inches from the backboard. Note that these measurements are standard for courts in the U.S.A. at this time. Note also that measurements will vary slightly depending whether you measure from the inside or outside of the line. See the diagram on the next page.

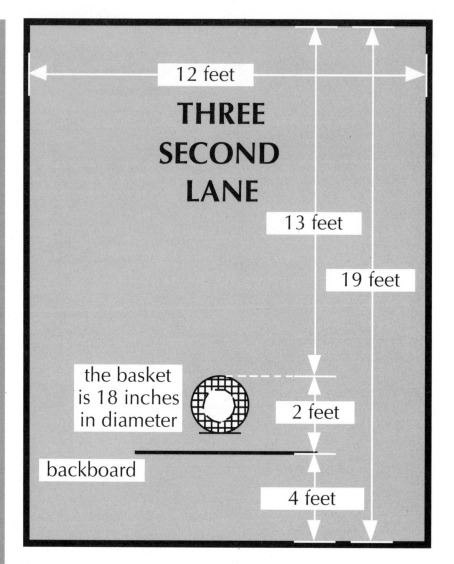

Areas

The three second lane contains the ***blood and guts*** **area**. Offensive and defensive players line up alternately on the lane for foul shots. The defense takes the position on the lane closest to the basket inside the innermost space mark. On offense, players can stay in the lane for a maximum of three seconds unless the ball is either shot or loose. Defensive players prevent the offense from having easy access to the lane. (12.4-12.6) To enter the lane unopposed, offensive players must fake and then make quick charges into this area for the ball. (10.5-10.7)

Other Terms

Backcourt – away from your own basket. Backcourt players are guards. In men's basketball, a backcourt violation occurs when a player crosses midcourt with the ball and then goes back.

Boards or off the boards – a rebound

Corner – the area directly to either side of the basket near the baseline. You can not use the backboard for corner shots.

Discontinuing – a dribbling violation; dribbling for a second time after stopping.

Double dribble – a dribbling violation; dribbling with 2 hands.

Forecourt and backcourt are not on the court. These are not specific locations. The forecourt is where the forwards play on offense. It is fore or closer to the basket than where the guards play. In a full court press when the guards take the ball out from the baseline, the forecourt could be near mid-court. In a regular offense the forecourt is around the basket and baseline. Farther away from the basket or back are the guards in the backcourt.

Foul line extended – walk on the foul line toward the left or right sideline. This area or line you walk on outside the foul line is the foul line extended area. With a paint brush you could extend the foul line to the sidelines. These extensions on the left and right sides are considered the foul line extended.

Free throw line – foul line

Give and go – Passing, then cutting to the basket (or other area) expecting to receive a return pass.

Head-to-head or belly-to-belly – play tight one-on-one defense.

Help out – moving into position to cover and covering another player's offensive assignment.

Inside –closer to the basket, usually in the lane. The defense usually takes an inside position. The offense always wants to pass inside.

In – in bounds; inside.

Man-to-man – archaic term for person-to-person defensive coverage.

On-off ball – On ball refers to defensive coverage on the ball. Off ball is the coverage on the other 4 players without the ball. On ball coverage is usually tight, whereas off ball coverage is usually much looser.

One-on-one – person-to-person defensive coverage.

Outside – farther from the basket. Teams do not want to take too many outside shots. Shorter players usually play outside.

Out–out-of-bounds; outside.

Over and back – a men's game violation; when you cross half court with the ball and then go back.

Paint – the three second lane. On most college and professional courts it is painted one color, often a color of the home team.

Palming – a dribbling violation when the palm of the dribbling hand is turned upward (and then downward) to better control the ball.

Ready position – a player's body position when on the court. The body should be in a half down position, feet shoulder width apart. Body weight is on the balls of the feet. Bending is from the knees, not the back. The fingers are spread apart, clawed. The ready positions for rebounding, defense, and offense are similar.

Screen or pick – when a stationary offensive player is used as, or sets up as, a block or impediment on the defensive player assigned to another offensive player. It is a violation if the screen moves to cause contact with the defense.

Shooting range or **range** – the maximum distance from which you can shoot well. Players often shoot from beyond their range.

Slough off – the defense moves away from the offense.

Strong- weak-side – The ball side of the court is called the strong side. The defense needs to guard closely here. The weak side is the off ball side of the court. The defense can slough off individual coverage and move toward the lane to help out.

The Lane – the 3 second lane.

Three second lane – the lane: the paint.

Tied up – when the offense is not able to pass or move the ball because the defense either gets their hands on the ball (jump ball) or prevents ball movement for 5 seconds (a violation).

Transition or **transition game** – moving from offense to defense or vice-versa. Players need to make quick transitions, especially from offense to defense.

Traveling – see "walking" below.

Violation – against the rules. The other team is awarded the ball out-of-bounds.

Walking – traveling; sliding the pivot foot while holding the ball or taking more than one-and-a-half steps while holding the ball. The half step is actually another step. Another way to say this is that it is a violation to take 2 full steps with the ball. When catching, a player takes the half step first. When passing or dribbling, the half step is the second step.

Chapter Three

3

Flow Chart of the Fundamentals

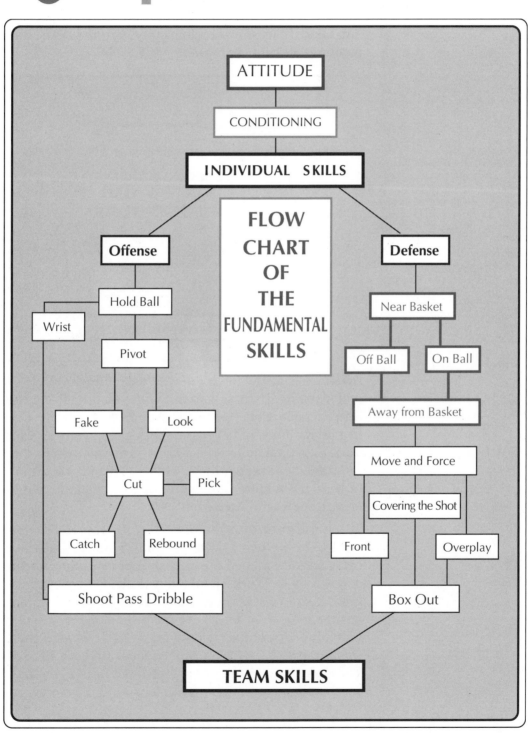

The Flow Chart

This flow chart introduces the fundamentals taught in the lessons. You can more easily recognize relationships between the skills in this form. The more basic ones, taught first, are at the top; more dependent and complex skills are further down. It is one way to look at the fundamentals. Lesson sections devoted to a particular skill are in parenthesis ( ) after the name. The table preceding this chapter lists all sections and lessons. Words from the chart like pivot, look, and fake are used interchangeably with the _ing_ ending- pivoting, looking, and faking.

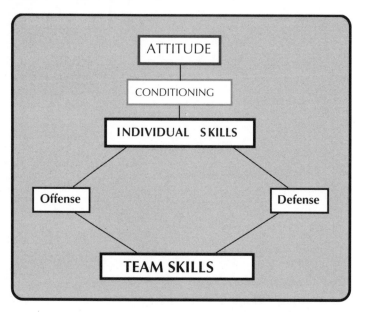

Attitude is at the top because it determines both the teaching and learning that transpires. What you do reflects your attitude, not what you say or even how you say it. *Conditioning* allows players to remain fresh enough to apply skills during the last quarter of a tight game. *Conditioning* also improves a player's athletic ability. This is at least as important as, if not more than, skill. Speed, strength, and quickness ensure successful execution.

Teach *individual offensive* (1-11,13) and *defensive* skills (12,13) before team skills (bottom). Planting individual seeds early permits immediate growth that continues during the entire season. Working on team skills postpones individual growth and wastes time and effort on things players are unprepared to do. There are more than double the number of individual *offensive* fundamentals as *defensive* ones. For this reason offense takes much longer to teach than defense. These skills are more intertwined and need to be taught separately before combined; defensive skills mostly require effort.

Offense

The offensive ball handling skills–shooting, passing, dribbling, catching–begin with ***Holding the ball*** (1). It is so simple–it takes only 5 minutes to teach–why bother mentioning it? Holding the ball properly not only positions the hands to catch the ball (the ready position), but also to shoot, pass, and dribble. Problem diagnosis in these areas start here. Another key, usually the missing key, to ball handling is ***wrist*** (3) movement. It is similar for shooting, passing, and dribbling even though the arms are in different positions.

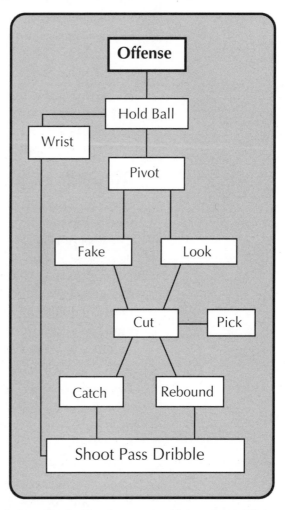

After acquiring the ball, players need to ***pivot*** (2) in order to shoot, pass, or dribble. Lacking pivoting expertise measurably detracts from all other skills. Two other commonly overlooked fundamentals are ***fake*** (parts of 6,8-10,12) and ***look*** or ***communication*** (parts of 10,12-19). *Faking* is the finishing touch that enables players to successfully execute any ***move***. Players fake with the ball, without the ball, and even on defense. ***Looking*** is something that coaches figure will just come naturally. Not so. It needs to be taught. All players must know where the ball is at all times as well as where the other players are. This includes dribblers, (especially) and passers, knowing who is behind them as well as in front. (Eyes behind the head are helpful.) **Looking** both to pass or before cutting involves much communication; it is not random. I've seen championships lost because players were not **looking** in the right place. Another key to offense, especially team offense, is **cutting** (10). Working against a press or attempting to pass or catch the ball inside involves a combination of **looking**, **faking**, and **cutting**. **Picking** or **screening** (13) involves **cutting** both to set the pick and to use it. Players, especially novices, **cutting** to the ball must stop running *after* **catching** (10) the ball; stopping *before* **catching** permits the defense an easy interception. For novices, a **catch** without walking after a cut to the ball is a difficult task.

Rebounding is another form of **catching** the ball with **cutting** and **looking** combined. Combine all of these offensive skills with shooting (5-8), passing (9), and dribbling (4), and you are ready to teach the team skills (14-19).

Defense

Even though defense (lessons 12-13) is most important to me, less practice time needs to be spent on it for many reasons. There is not only less to learn, but also many offensive lessons develop skills used in defense (not because defense is played in the lesson). All conditioning lessons help as well because defense is 90% effort. All dribbling lessons help defense because dribbling position is similar to defensive position. You may have noticed that good dribblers are usually good on defense. For the reasons mentioned above, a team's defensive play usually varies less than its offense.

Defense is most important **near the basket** because this area is the easiest place to score. I estimate that teams shoot over 80% within 3 feet of the basket compared to less than 50% overall. Defending the **blood and guts area** is the key to team defense. Games are won or lost there.

One-on-one coverage of the player with the ball is not as important as you think, though it is important. Only one player is **on** the ball while four are **off**, away from the ball. Any offensive player can beat one defender. However, it is difficult for one player to beat five players if the other four help out. **Off ball** defenders prevent the offense from taking advantage of the defense. They also close down access to the **blood and guts area**.

The main defensive skill is **move and force** (12), which includes **fronting** (12), **overplaying** (12), and **covering the**

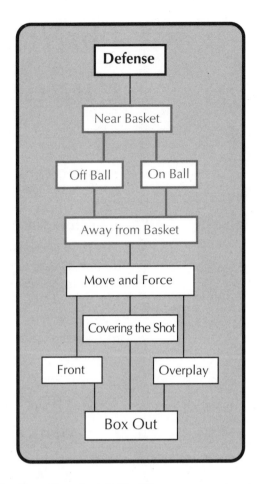

shot or defending the shot (12). ***Move*** means to stay with (or one step ahead of) the offense with or without the ball. ***Force*** a player with the ball either to the opposite hand or to the sidelines while dribbling down court, or to the center of the court near the basket. ***Fronting*** (face-guarding) involves playing the offense face-to-face (belly-to-belly is a more apt description). Covering both the ball and players during out-of-bounds plays, as well as in ***boxing out,*** are situations where fronting is used. ***Overplaying*** is used to cover players without the ball. The objective is to prevent passes, cuts near the basket, and offensive rebounding. ***Covering*** the shot means to set up properly on players with the ball when they are in scoring position. Most often the defense should force players in the center of the court to their opposite hand; force players on the sides to the center toward help, since there usually is no help on the baseline. Players ***box out*** after shots whether they are ***fronting***, ***overplaying***, or ***covering the shot.***

Chapter Four
4

Outline of the Fundamentals

This outline complements the flow chart. It presents relationships between the skills in more detail. The main headings are Practice or Pregame Skills, Individual Skills, and Team Skills. The next chapter discusses these topics even though the outline could stand on its own. Read through it.

The first section on practice and pregame skills are those that do not fit into the other categories. Most of this outline involves individual skills, Section II. I divide it into four parts–non-ball skills, ball skills, going-for-the-ball skills, and defensive skills. The last section on team skills presents half and full court setups as well as ways players should react in each situation.

THE TEACHABLE SKILLS

I. Practice or Pregame Skills

A. Attitude
1. Teaching
2. Winning
3. Recruiting

B. Conditioning
1. Cardiovascular
2. Body–Legs, Trunk, Arms

C. Warm-Up and Warm Down

D. Hustle

E. Game Procedures
1. Reporting In and Out
2. Bench Behavior

II. Individual Skills

A. Offensive Non-Ball Skills
1. Looking & Communication

      a. Locate Ball at All Times

      b. Where to Cut

      c. Where to Pass

      d. Out-of-Bounds Plays

      e. Deception–Before Passing, Cutting, Stealing

      f. Dribbling

      g. Team Looking on Defense

   2. Pivoting

   3. Faking

      a. With Body, Head, Eyes, Ball

      b. Before Passing, Dribbling, Cutting, Shooting

   4. Occupying the Defense

   5. Picking or Screening

B. Individual Ball Skills

   1. Holding the Ball

   2. Wrist Skills

      a. Dribbling

      b. Shooting

      c. Passing

   3. Moves

      a. Around the Basket

      b. To the Basket

      c. Before Shooting

C. Going-for-the-ball Skills

   1. Catching

   2. Cutting

   3. Loose Ball

   4. Rebounding

D. Individual Defensive Skills

   1. Body Position

   2. On Ball-Covering the Ball

      a. Near Basket

      b. 12 Feet Away

         (1) Near Side Lines

         (2) Near or In Lanes

      c. Near Midcourt

3. Off Ball–Preventing Catches & Cuts
   a. Techniques
      (1) Fronting
      (2) Overplaying
      (3) Backing
   b. Low Post (and Boxing Out)
   c. High Post
   d. Out-of-Bounds Play
   e. Cutters
4. Preventing Rebounds–Boxing Out

III. Team Skills

A. Center Jump

B. Transition Game
1. From the Foul Line
2. From the Center Jump

C. Offense Against
1. Zones
2. Person-to-Person Defense

D. Defense
1. Helping Out
2. Zones
3. Playing the Pick

E. Out-of-Bounds Plays

F. Full and Half Court Pressure

Chapter Five

5

Discussion of the Fundamentals

•Note that the table of lessons from **The Basketball Coach's Bible** follows this chapter, so you can better follow the lesson references. Some references are in parenthesis.

Practice or Pregame Skills

Attitude

This book reflects my attitude and ideas because it describes what I did. I explain the things that work well. Many more things did not work well; that is another book. In the Do Not section of the **Principles of Practice Teaching** chapter I describe some of these field-tested mistakes.

Whenever I was uncertain of what to do or how to handle players, I kept three things in mind:

> **1.** Teach each individual as though everything depends on it. (It does.) Do what is best for each individual; this is what is best for the team.

> **2.** Minimize differences among players.

> **3.** Be specific when talking to players; don't waste their time; no BSing.

In the end, your players will reflect your attitude.

Every jock and good ole boy (or girl) adage that I have ever heard reflects an attitude antithetical to teaching. I must comment on one in particular. I am not unaffected by these ideas and speak from experience.

"Winning is the only thing" declares this famous, widely quoted (or misquoted) sports proverb. This idea encourages coaches to judge both their team's and their own individual success based on winning and losing. "We won, so we must have played well. I also did a great job coaching and planning." Or "We lost, we need more practice. I must work harder." None of this is necessarily correct. Coaches need a more concrete basis for evaluation. Thinking this way there is none.

Winning also becomes a moral issue. Winners are good in every sense–good in basketball, good as people, morally righteous. Losers are folks that are no good in every way and, further, do not deserve any consideration. Try to get a job in competition with the home town star. Often the poorer players on a team are invisible or are considered lesser people.

The coach thinks, "Why spend time with a player who will not help me win?" Good players yield good or worthwhile people. We will spend the time to make sure they get to class and pass the algebra test.

Winning also corrupts. If winning is the only thing, what is to prevent illegal and unethical actions to achieve this end? I've too often seen recruiting violations, pacts between coaches and referees, corruption among timers and official scorers, and, in general, too many non-game related things done to take advantage of others.

How many times were you angry at players in practice or a game for making a mistake? Winning demands players do things right whether or not they know how. **Teaching** says that the only limit to a player's ability to learn is the teacher's ability to teach. Face it, players' mistakes stem from your inabilities. **Teaching** encourages coaches to study basketball and to examine themselves; it is giving of yourself, whereas winning only demands, takes, and uses.

Winning paradoxically always makes you a big loser because nobody wins all the time. Only one team wins the championship. All the others lose. On the other hand, when you **teach** you win all the time. **Every practice and every game are wins if your players learn.** This book shows you how to be a winner in a real sense. It will also inadvertently help you score more points than the other team.

My most satisfying day as a coach was neither the day we won the city championship nor when we won games against favored opponents. I was absent on my most satisfying day as a coach. My captain ran a practice that we had planned and discussed the previous day since I knew I would be absent. Another coach in the gym said *the players practiced as if I were there.* This may not sound like much to you, but it means everything to me; my practices are tough.

Conditioning

In the recipe for successful coaching, *conditioning* is one of the most important ingredients. I notice that players often tire in the second half, particularly near the end of the game. The conditioned team gets all those loose balls; the tired team is much slower. The conditioned team has an easier time on offense and continues to play tight defense; tired teams do not think well, execute directions well, play tight defense, or even shoot well. There is no match between tired and conditioned teams. I have seen better skilled and more talented tired teams lose to lesser conditioned teams innumerable times at the high school and college level.

So, one objective that is pervasive throughout every practice is conditioning. Explain this to your players just as I have done above. How do you condition your players in a time efficient and effective way? The answer is surprisingly simple—a continuous movement or motion lesson. Lessons 1.2 and 1.3 are examples.

A continuous movement lesson means just that. Players do not stop moving or running at any time during the lesson. The skills involved in these lessons are often the same ones that you want to teach. Initially they involve the basic ball handling skills. Add practice shooting and team skills to these lessons as well. As the season progresses you can find a way to make any lesson continuous motion.

At the beginning of the season, we move for 15 minutes and then gradually work up to 30 minutes. Adjust this to the condition of your players. We want long-term cardiovascular conditioning, not anaerobic or sprinting activities; many other lessons involve sprinting. A great mistake is to force out of shape players to go faster; just keep them moving. A thoroughbred will run at a very fast pace whereas a heavy player will barely move. It takes time to get in shape; injury takes little time. Players greatly strengthen their legs as well in these drills.

Here are three instructive examples of how to and not to get in shape.

1. A friend always had trouble getting in shape. He ran hard. He was always out of breath. His feet would be bloody after running around the track. His legs would be sore. It always worked this way, and it was nearly impossible for him to improve his condition. He always just gave up or had to quit because of pain and injury.

2. George, a friend's brother, wanted to get in shape. I went out jogging with him. I walked, he jogged. Since this was his first time jogging, I told him not to jog faster than I was walking. We had an enjoyable conversation while exercising for about 10 minutes. He said it was difficult to go that slowly. I told him it was the only way to start without injury. Less than a year later I ran into George's brother who told me that George was running 9 miles a day.

3. When I get in shape, I go slowly. I go from 0 minutes to 1 hour of jogging per day without injury, stiffness, or even getting much out of breath. If I am out of shape, I just walk for an hour or so a day. In one case I remember being totally out of shape before going on a trip to England. During the first three weeks there, I walked all day around London, Edinburgh, and the Lake District. At Oxford I met some friends who wanted to go for a jog around the area. I warned them of my poor condition, that I would need to go slowly and even then I could not last long. We jogged for over 45 minutes. I had no difficulty breathing and no soreness afterward. I had walked myself into shape.

There is a phrase too often used in sports about conditioning that I must comment on. Every one has heard it or used it– "NO PAIN, NO GAIN." Pain is often a warning sign to your body that you are overdoing it. Overdoing it causes stiffness and injury. It is a step backward because it puts you out-of-business. Sensible conditioning gets you where you want to go without injury. There is no choice - *easy does it* all the way. Adding to this well-known credo places it in its rightful context–*No Pain, No Gain, No Brain*.

All sports mottoes have one thing in common. They substitute emotion in place of planning. It is easier to spit out trite mottoes urging your players to victory than to study basketball. It is easier to blame players for their poor play than to spend more time planning your practice. A new motto to replace some old ones is *Plan Hard, Improve Much*. We need to spread around some sensible ones. Please send them to me. See the address on the order form at the back of this book.

Warm-Up and Warm Down

You do not need a special warm-up. Any moderately paced movement loosens muscles; even shooting around before practice will do. The continuous motion lesson is also a good warm-up. Stretching tight muscles before they are loose can cause injury. On the other hand, after practice leg muscles are loose and will tighten up. Stretching after practice prevents this. It is also a good time for players to cool off before going outside. A player leads the lesson while you talk to your players; plant ideas, give homework and reminders. Appendix B presents a warm down.

Hustle

Hustle is another skill that many think you **just can't teach**. Nothing is further from the truth; it is easy to teach. It takes no talent to learn. Some of the many lessons that teach hustle include *Go Fetch-It (10.1), Catch-Up (7.2), Fronting (12.4),*

Overplaying (12.5), all transition lessons, etc. Hustle lessons are part of the everyday practice. Every player I have coached learned to hustle.

Game Procedures

Experience taught me that novice players need practice reporting into and out of games. Once it took several minutes during a scrimmage to corral a group of replaced players who continued to play. Rehearse reporting in and out.

Avoid substitution problems in a game by informing the substituted players ahead of time. Advise him/her to watch the player being replaced. Before reporting in *the player tells you* the offensive and defensive positions.

Practice bench behavior, especially with younger players. Some simple rules are:

> **1.** Players always remain on the bench always when not in the game. No going for water or anywhere else without permission.
>
> **2.** Fans root, players control themselves despite what some pros and college players do.
>
> **3.** During time outs, bench players give up their seats to those in the game. Then they form a semicircle around you so they can easily hear the directions and you can more readily talk, if there is a noisy crowd.

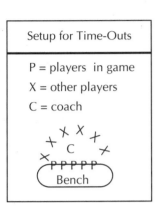

Setup for Time-Outs

P = players in game
X = other players
C = coach

Offensive Non-Ball Skills

Looking and Communication

These are both teachable, distinct fundamentals taught in tandem with others. Usually coaches do not teach these skills because they do not perceive them as skills.

Whether on offense or defense, each player must always know where the ball is; this involves *looking.* Many defensive lessons, involving strong- and weak-side play and overplaying, emphasize watching (*looking* at) both the ball and the offense. In addition, defensive players must watch (*look*) for cutting, especially near the basket. Rebounding also involves *looking* at shot arcs to predict where the ball will go.

On offense *looking* means more than watching the ball; it is directed, not random. Players evaluate situations to find openings. Always look to pass inside. Look long in out-of-bounds plays under the opponent's basket even before picking up the ball; look short under your own basket. Passers and dribblers especially must be aware of everything both in front and behind them. Communicating to another player a cut or pass to a particular spot are other *looking* skills incorporated into many lessons. Some of these are 9.51, 9.52, 10.61.

Pivoting

The first move after a player touches a ball is a pivot. Picking up a loose ball, rebounding, catching a pass, driving, shooting, or dribbling all involve pivoting. A lack of ability to pivot affects a player's ability to perform all the above tasks. One can never practice enough pivoting. Eventually players practice it in tandem with all other skills. See section 2.

Faking

The difference in the effectiveness of much of what we do depends on *faking*. Players *fake* before passing, shooting, dribbling, or cutting. On defense as well, players *fake* to steal passes or a dribbled ball. Players fake with the ball, head, eyes, and/or body.

One big difference between skilled and unskilled players is the ability to fake. This discrepancy only happens because faking is usually not taught, even though it is not an advanced skill. Lesson 10.5 teaches faking separately, whereas lessons 6.0-6.6 (plus others) teach faking in tandem with other skills. Inexperienced players can readily learn and use fakes.

Offense Off the Ball

A player without the ball on offense (4 of 5 players) either wants to hide or be seen intentionally by the defense. Both of these involve *faking*. See 10.5.

•To be seen is easier. The player's objective is to occupy the eyes and attention of the defense. This prevents the defense from helping out on the ball. To accomplish this distraction players overtly act as if they want the ball or are going to cut to the basket. Stay in view; fake cuts away from the ball.

•The offense *hides* before a cut to the ball so that the defense cannot react quickly to the play. A player accomplishes this move several ways:

> **1.** Stay out of the normal view of the defense. Move to the side or behind the defense.

> **2.** Act like you are sleeping, not paying attention to the game.

The offense should do both. The defense either does not see or ignores the offense.

Screening or Picking

Screening is important when the defense is strong. This is rarely the case with young players. Therefore, screening is one of the last skills taught (section 13). Players often use picks in two situations:

1. When the defense is person-to-person
2. During out-of-bounds plays.

Individual Ball Skills

Holding the Ball

One of the most overlooked skills is *holding the ball*. It is a prerequisite to learning all the ball handling skills, such as shooting, passing and catching, and dribbling. For this reason it is the first lesson. Novice and other players exhibiting problems with any ball handling skill need only a few minutes of instruction. I heard somewhere and others have confirmed the fact that one former great NBA shooter, Pete Maravitch, slept holding the ball.

This first lesson will immediately help the many players labelled *butterfingers*, who have difficulty catching the ball. Difficulty catching the ball often leads these players to be afraid of it. They turn away from hard passes or attempt to catch passes with their eyes shut. As a result they often injure fingers in the attempt to catch the ball, and they rarely catch the ball. This is all for naught.

Examine how a butterfingered player holds the ball: by using much of the palms and lower parts of the fingers. To control the ball, players need to hold it with the ***fingertips***, not palms. Only the fingertips touch the ball. (The term *touch,* as in shooting *touch,* alludes to this.) Try catching a ball the butterfingered way with your palms. Have your players try this as well. It is difficult, if not impossible.

The first step of the correct way to catch the ball involves making the hands into claws. Hold the ball in these claws with contact only at the fingertips. The first lesson, 1.0, details this.

Wrist Skills

Shooting (5,7,8), passing (9), and dribbling (4) are wrist skills, because the fluid motion of the wrist along with the hand is the major limiting factor to improvement. Before practicing any ball skills, 1-2 minutes of wrist work pays off in great dividends. Besides making the motion more fluid, it also strengthens the wrist. Improvement can occur without even touching the ball. (3.0)

The wrist skills are the most difficult ones to learn, in part because they involve the entire body, not just the wrists. Players need much coordination to perform them well. In addition, coaches rarely teach these skills. Often coaches use naturally talented players in lieu of teaching this skill and then readily claim, "*You just can't teach it.*" Every shooting lesson that I have read or watched was academic in nature (even the Wizard of Westwood, John Wooden, did it that way in a video); a beautiful explanation at best. Nowhere do coaches give players a way or technique to practice. Nowhere do coaches break the skills down into learnable parts. The obvious fact that even some pros (Hall of Famers too) do not have the technique of well-instructed 9th graders attests to the horrendous state of teaching. This applies to passing and dribbling as well.

Start teaching the wrist skills immediately so players can practice them correctly on their own.

Moves

A *move* is what I call a more advanced scoring skill, although coaches, as well as I, often use this term more broadly to mean any series of movements. The purpose of all moves is to score. Moves are often considered *slick* since they fake out the defense. Players often invent them during games, making it difficult to present them all. The section on *moves* (6) gives players a varied sample.

Going-for-the-Ball Skills

Catching (10), cutting (10), going for loose balls (10+), and rebounding (11) are the *going for the ball skills*. All of these skills involve looking to start, hustle in the middle, and pivoting to end. In between, players use many other skills such as positioning, communicating, and grabbing the ball. Moving quickly helps also.

The most difficult part of catching involves cutting to the ball or to the open space. Practicing catching lessons without cutting is for naught. With the defense close, the player that catches the ball is the one who moves to the ball one step ahead of the opponent. Teams with *going-for-the-ball-skills* beat presses.

Rebounding is another *going-for-the-ball* skill not often taught. The keys to rebounding involve predicting where the ball will go and then moving to the best position. Section 11 divides rebounding into teachable parts.

Individual Defensive Skills

Defense (section 12) is easier to teach than offense because it is mostly physical; it takes little talent to learn. There are fewer defensive skills than offensive ones to master. Each skill is less complicated as well, so players learn much faster than offense. A team's shooting often varies from game to game, but the defense can be more constant, something you can rely on.

Often coaches forgo teaching person-to-person defense because the coach thinks, incorrectly, that a zone defense is easier to learn. Even in a zone players need to cover the player with the ball one-on-one. Under the boards the defense again must play low post players one-on-one. Each situation in a zone ends up with the defense playing the offense one-on-one. Zone players, in addition, need to know how the zone shifts. For these reasons zones are more difficult to teach and learn, not easier than one-on-one defense.

Most of the opponents' zones that my teams faced were only places for players to stand on the court. Any particular defensive player seemed to have no idea how to cover the player with the ball. Coaches need to teach players how to play one-on-one rather than where to stand on the court.

Some problems may arise using person-to-person defense. With inexperienced players you are more vulnerable under the boards since the players are not *all milling around there* as in most zones. Novice players also muddle the coverage by losing the player they are guarding or by picking up the wrong player. However, in the long run your players will do better than you would ever expect. They learn how to play defense, not take up space.

I break down individual defensive skills into four basic categories:

1. Body position
2. On ball–covering the ball
3. Off ball–preventing catches & cuts
4. Preventing rebounds

Body position is **the defensive position**. This position facilitates quick, fast movements in any direction. The body is low with feet shoulder-width apart. Lesson 12.0 gives the details.

Covering the ball means to cover the offensive player with the ball in any position on the court. **The keys to learning this skill are the Three Yard and Forcing lessons (12.1-12.2)** These teach a player to stay in the best defensive position one step ahead of the offense. Covering the shooter is another skill often not taught. Most players just attempt to block the shot, flailing their arms around the shooter. Often referees call a foul whether or not there is contact. (12.7)

In a person-to-person defense only one player covers the ball. Four work to prevent the offense from catching it where they want. Overplaying (12.5) and fronting (12.4) teach this important skill.

Treat any offensive player going into the **blood and guts area** or already there very specially. In particular, prevent offensive rebounders coming from behind the basket. Lesson 12.6 combines fronting, overplaying, and boxing out in this area.

Team Skills

Individual skills make up most of the teachable skills. There are few team skills compared to the individual ones, or at least fewer than most people think. Team skills most importantly coordinate the movements of all players. They furnish players a court position from which they execute individual skills. However, players need to know *how to do it* well before they need to know *where to do it.*. That is why team skills, in my opinion, take a back seat to the individual ones. Even though I present a minimum of team skills, there is still enough here for a professional team.

The team skills include the center jump (14), the foul line setup and transition game (15), half court offensive (16) and defensive (17) setups, out-of-bounds plays (18), and full and half court pressure setups (19). Often I went into preseason games before teaching many team skills. I never taught zone defense in practice. However, I once did during a game. It took only one time out for the players to learn how to play an excellent shifting 2-1-2 zone defense. These were inexperienced 10th graders. They even surprised me.

Games start with a center jump, so teach it first. I have even taught it at the start of a preseason scrimmage. Teaching detailed center jump plays is a poor use of time especially since it is only used a few times a game. A simple defensive jump setup prevents you from "getting burned." Trickier plays can evolve with developing communication during the season.

The foul line setup is a great way to teach boxing out as well as the transition game skills. The transition game involves going from offense to defense or vice-versa quickly. It is one team skill that players need before the first scrimmage. You may find that shooting from the foul line may be difficult for novices. So, move novices closer to the basket. Shooting from too far destroys shooting technique. As shooting technique develops allow players to move back closer to the foul line.

The keys to team offense are:

1. Cutting to the open space

2. Communication between the passer and cutter.

Practice these as individual skills, not as part of practice plays. They take much time to learn. Keep offenses simple like *Plays 1,2,3* in Lesson 16.1. Guidelines for any practice play are:

1. The ending is a short shot or layup

2. All players go for the rebound

3. There is a transition made to the defense.

The most complex combination of the individual and team skills involves pressure offense against a pressure defense. Teach it as soon as your players are ready, not before.

COACH'S TABLE OF LESSONS

Table Explanation

All table features are discussed in more detail in other sections and are also part of each lesson.

Lesson # and Name

The lessons are listed in order with the first lesson in each section in bold. The name of the first lesson in each section denotes the type of skill involved.

Players

The players needed in each group involved in the lesson. Note that the directions are given for many groups.

Court and Ball

X means you need a court or a ball for this lesson. A dash (-) means you do not.

Effort Level

1=little physical activity, technique level lesson

2=moderate activity, practice level

3=maximum physical effort involved, game level

Lessons Before

These lessons are needed before you do the current one. Usually only the lesson before is needed. However, sometimes many other lessons are needed, and it would be difficult to complete the current lesson without them.

Intro Time and Daily Time

The Intro Time is the time needed to teach a lesson for the first time. Usually it is double the Daily Time, the time needed after players understand the lesson.

Coach's Table of Lessons

L E S S O N #	NAME	P L A Y E R S	C O U R T	B A L L	E F F O R T	LESSONS BEFORE	L E S S O N #	INTRO TIME	DAILY TIME
1.0	**Holding the Ball**	1	-	x	1	none	**1.0**	5-10	1-2
1.1	Take Away	2	-	x	1	1.0	1.1	5-10	1-5
1.11	Hold High	2	-	x	1	1.1	1.11	-	1-5
1.12	Hold Low	2	-	x	1	1.1	1.12	-	1-5
1.2	Grab Full Court	2	x	x	2	1.1, 5.4	1.2	10-20	10-20
1.21	Short Pass Full Court	2	x	x	2	1.2	1.21	-	10-20
1.22	Tricky Pass Full Court	2	x	x	2	1.2	1.22	-	10-20
1.3	Line Lesson	T	x	x	2-3	1.1, 1.2	1.3	15-55	5-15
1.4	Move Ball	2	-	x	3	1.1	1.4	5-10	2-5
2.0	**Start Pivoting**	1	-	-	1	none	**2.0**	10-15	5-10
2.1	Pivoting with Ball	1	-	x	2	1.0, 2.0	2.1	15-20	2-20
2.2	Pivot with Defense	2	-	x	3	1.4, 2.1, 7.1	2.2	15-20	5-10
2.21	Pivot with D Pass	2+	x	x	3	2.2	2.21	10	5-10
2.22	Pivot 2 on D	3	x	x	3	2.21	2.22	10	5-10
2.23	Pivot 2 on D Pass	3+	x	x	3	2.22	2.23	10	5-10
3.0	**Flick of the Wrist - Shoot, Pass, Dribble**	1	-	-	1	none	**3.0**	10-15	2
4.0	**Dribbling D Position**	1	-	x	1	3.0	**4.0**	5-10	1-2
4.1	Look at the Leader 1-2	1+	x	x	2	4.0	4.1	20-30	5-15
4.11	Look and Count	1+	-	x	2	4.1	4.11	"	"
4.12	Watch the Game	1+	-	x	2	4.1	4.12	-	-
4.13	Twist Around	1	-	x	2	4.1	4.13	-	5-15
4.2	Follow the Leader	1+	-	x	2	4.1, 4.13	4.2	15-20	5-15
4.21	Follow Step Ahead	1+	-	x	2	4.2	4.21	-	5-15
4.22	Follow Back & Sideways	1+	-	x	2	4.2	4.22	-	1-5
4.23	Twister	1	-	-	2	4.22	4.23	5-10	1-5
4.24	Twister with Ball	1	-	x	2	4.23	4.24	-	5-10
4.3	Protect Ball	2	-	x	2-3	4.2	4.3	10-25	5-10
4.31	Protect with 2 on D	3	-	x	3	4.3	4.31	-	5-10
4.32	Dribbler Vs Dribbler	2	-	x	2	4.3	4.32	-	10-20
4.4	Dribble with D Layup	1+	x	x	2-3	4.3, 5.41	4.4	15-25	10-20
4.5	Dribble Pass with D	3	-	x	3	4.4, 9.3, 9.6, 10.5	4.5	20-30	10-20
4.51	Dribbler Shoots Ball	3	x	x	3	4.5	4.51	-	10-20
4.52	With D on Cutter	4	x	x	3	4.5	4.52	-	10-20
5.0	**Shot Technique Wrists**	1	-	-	1	none	**5.0**	10-15	2
5.1	Flick Up	1	-	x	1	5.0	5.1	10-20	2-5
5.11	Opposite Hand Flick Up	1	-	x	1	5.1	5.11	-	2-5
5.12	Flick Up High	1	-	x	1	5.1	5.12	-	2-4
5.13	Shoot Up	1	-	x	2	5.12	5.13	-	1-2
5.2	One-Inch Shot	1	x	x	1	5.13	5.2	10-30	5-10
5.3	One-Foot Shot	1	x	x	2	5.2	5.3	10-20	5-15
5.31	Regular One-Foot Shot	1	x	x	2	5.3	5.31	-	5-10
5.32	One-Foot Shot +Dribble	1+	x	x	2	4.3	5.32	-	5-15
5.33	One-Foot Jump Shot	1+	x	x	2	5.31	5.33	-	5-10

Coach's Table of Lessons continued

LESSON #	NAME	PLAYERS	COURT	BALL	EFFORT	LESSONS BEFORE	LESSON #	INTRO TIME	DAILY TIME
5.4	The No-Step Layup	1	x	x	1	1.0	5.4	15-30	5-20
5.41	One-Step Layup	1	x	x	1	5.4	5.41	-	5-20
5.42	Layup Lesson	T	x	x	2	5.41	5.42	10-20	10-15
5.43	Layup with Dribble	1	x	x	2	4.2, 5.42	5.43	15-20	5-15
5.44	Layup with Passing	T	x	x	2	5.42, 9.1	5.44	15-25	5-15
5.5	One Dribble Layup	1	x	x	2	4.2, 5.42	5.5	15-25	5-15
5.51	Two Dribble Layup	1	x	x	2	5.5	5.51	-	5-15
5.6	Foul Shot Technique	1	-	x	1	5.3	5.6	10-15	2-5
5.61	Technique Short Shot	1	-	x	1	5.6	5.61	10-15	5-15
5.62	Technique Longer Shots	1	-	x	1	5.61	5.62	-	5-15
5.7	Foul Shot Practice	1	x	x	3	5.6	5.7	5-15	5-15
5.8	Lateral Layup Lesson	T	x	x	2	2.1, 5.43, 9.5, 10.61	5.8	15-25	5-15
5.81	Bounce Pass Layup	T	x	x	2	5.8	5.81	-	5-15
6.0	**Moves**	x	x	x	-	2.1, 5.3	**6.0**	5-15	0-20
6.1	Pivot Around Shoot	1	x	x	2	6.0	6.1	5-15	0-20
6.2	Pivot Backward Shoot	1	x	x	2	6.1	6.2	5-15	0-20
6.3	Step Fake Shoot	1	x	x	2	6.0	6.3	5-15	0-20
6.31	Fake Pivot Shoot	1	x	x	2	6.3	6.31	5-15	0-20
6.32	Fake Pivot Back Shoot	1	x	x	2	6.31	6.32	5-15	0-20
6.4	Pivot Fake Shoot	1	x	x	2	6.0	6.4	5-15	0-20
6.41	Pivot Fake Back Shoot	1	x	x	2	6.4	6.41	5-15	0-20
6.5	Hook Shot 1-2	1	x	x	2	6.0	6.5	5-15	0-20
6.51	Jump Hook	1	x	x	2	6.5	6.51	5-15	0-20
6.52	Hook with Fake	1	x	x	2	6.51	6.52	5-15	0-20
6.53	Step Hook	1	x	x	2	6.51	6.53	5-15	0-20
6.54	Fake Step Hook	1	x	x	2	6.52-3	6.54	5-15	0-20
6.55	Underneath Hooks	1	x	x	2	6.54	6.55	5-15	0-20
6.6	Jump Shot	1	x	x	2	6.0	6.6	5-15	0-20
6.61	Fake Jump	1	x	x	2	6.6	6.61	5-15	0-20
6.62	Fake Pivot Around Jump	1	x	x	2	6.61	6.62	5-15	0-20
6.63	Pump Fake	1	x	x	2	6.6	6.63	5-10	5-10
7.0	**Pressure Shot**	1	x	x	2-3	6.1 or 6.6	**7.0**	5-15	5-15
7.01	Pressure Shot with D	2	x	x	3	7.0	7.01	-	5-15
7.02	Pressure Shot Two	2	x	x	3	7.01, 10.3, 11.0	7.02	-	5-15
7.1	Run Stop Shoot	1	x	x	2-3	6.6	7.1	5-10	2-5
7.11	With D	2	x	x	3	7.1	7.11	-	2-5
7.12	Run Catch Shoot	2	x	x	3	7.1, 9.1 10.6	7.12	10-20	5-15
7.2	Catch Up	2	x	x	3	5.51, 7.0	7.2	5-10	5
7.3	Defense in Face Shoot	2	x	x	3	5.3	7.3	5-10	2-5
7.31	Defense in Face Rebound	2	x	x	3	7.3, 11.3	7.31	-	2-5
7.32	Fouled Shooting	1	x	x	3	7.3	7.32	-	2-5
8.0	**Practice Shooting**	-	x	x	-	-	**8.0**	-	-
8.1	Driving to the Basket	1	x	x	2	2.1, 5.51	8.1	10-15	5
8.11	Fake Then Drive	1	x	x	2	6.4, 8.1	8.11	5-10	5

Coach's Table of Lessons continued

LESSON #	NAME	PLAYERS	COURT	BALL	EFFORT	LESSONS BEFORE	LESSON #	INTRO TIME	DAILY TIME
8.12	Drive Opposite Foot	1	x	x	2	8.1	8.12	5-10	5
8.2	Full Court Shoot	1	x	x	2	4.24, 6.6, 8.1	8.2	5-10	5-15
8.3	Near to Far	1	x	x	2	5.62	8.3	-	5-15
9.0	**Passing Technique**	1	-	-	1	2.0, 3.0	**9.0**	5	1-2
9.1	Overhead Short Pass	2	-	x	1-2	9.0, 10.0	9.1	5-10	5
9.11	Side Short Pass	2	-	x	1-2	9.1	9.11	-	5
9.12	Bounce Pass	2	-	x	1-2	9.1	9.12	-	5
9.13	Pivot Away Back Pass	2	-	x	1-2	2.1, 9.1	9.13	-	5
9.2	Baseball Pass	2	x	x	2	none	9.2	5-10	5
9.3	Baseball Pass Cut	2	x	x	2	7.1, 9.2	9.3	10-15	5-10
9.31	Midcourt Cut	2	x	x	2	9.3	9.31	-	5-10
9.32	Continuous Half Court	T	x	x	2	9.31	9.32	-	5-10
9.4	Continuous Full Court	T	x	x	2	7.2, 9.3	9.4	20-30	10-20
9.41	Full Court Pass	T	x	x	2	9.4	9.41	20-30	10-30
9.5	Pivot Pass & Communication	2	-	x	2	2.1, 9.1, 10.0	9.5	10-15	5-10
9.51	Pass Communication	2	-	x	2	9.5	9.51	10-15	5
9.52	Communication 2	2	-	x	2	9.51	9.52	-	5
9.6	D Overhead Side Pass	3	-	x	2-3	2.2, 9.51, 12.0	9.6	12-25	5-10
9.61	Defense Bounce Pass	3	-	x	2-3	9.6	9.61	-	5-10
9.7	Front Weave	3	x	x	2	5.8	9.7	15-20	10
9.8	Back Weave	T	-	x	2	1.1	9.8	10-15	5
10.0	**Catch Cut Technique**	1+	-	x	1	1.0, 9.0	**10.0**	10-20	5-10
10.01	Catching Technique 2	2	-	x	1	10.0	10.01	-	5-10
10.1	"Go Fetch It"	1+	-	x	1-2	10.0	10.1	5-20	2-10
10.11	Coming to the Ball	1+	-	x	1-2	10.1	10.11	5-10	5-10
10.2	Jump to Ball	2	-	x	1-2	10.0	10.2	10-15	5-10
10.3	Loose Ball Lesson	2	-	x	3	1.1, 11.2	10.3	5-10	3-5
10.31	Go for It	2+	-	x	3	10.3	10.31	-	3-5
10.4	Catching Bad Passes	1+	-	x	2	10.2	10.4	3-8	2-5
10.5	Cut Fake Technique	1	-	-	1	none	10.5	10-20	5-15
10.51	Cutting Off A Pick	3	-	-	1	10.5	10.51	10-20	5-15
10.6	Cut to the Ball	2	-	x	2	10.2, 10.5	10.6	10-20	5-15
10.61	Cut Communication	2	x	x	2	10.6	10.61	10-20	5-15
10.7	Three Second Lesson	1	x	-	1	10.2, 10.5	10.7	3-6	3-4
10.71	Cut into Lane	2	x	x	2	10.2	10.71	10-15	5-10
10.8	Overplay the Catcher	2	x	x	3	9.5, 10.6, 12.5	10.8	10-20	5-20
10.81	Front the Catcher	3	x	x	3	9.5, 10.6, 12.4	10.81	10-20	5-20
10.82	D on Catcher, Cut	3	x	x	3	10.8	10.82	-	5-15
10.9	D Pass, Overplay Catch	4	x	x	3	9.6, 10.82	10.9	5-20	5-15
10.91	D Passer, Front Catch	4	x	x	3	9.6, 10.81	10.91	5-10	5-15
10.92	D on Catcher,Passer Cut	4	x	x	3	10.82-10.91	10.92	5-20	5-15
11.0	**Rebound Grab Ball**	2	x	-	1	1.1, 2.1	**11.0**	5-10	2-5
11.1	Watching the Ball	1	-	-	1	none	11.1	5-10	5
11.11	The Ready Position	1	-	-	1	11.1	11.11	3	1

Coach's Table of Lessons continued

L E S S O N #	NAME	P L A Y E R S	C O U R T	B A L L	E F F O R T	LESSONS BEFORE	L E S S O N #	INTRO TIME	DAILY TIME
11.12	Move to Rebound	1	-	-	1	11.1	11.12	5	5
11.2	Step in Front Box Out 1-2	2	x	x	3	10.3, 11.12	11.2	10-15	5-10
11.3	Blocking Boxing Out 1-2	2	x	x	3	11.2, 12.5	11.3	15-30	10-20
12.0	**Defensive Position**	1	-	-	1	4.0	**12.0**	10-20	2-4
12.1	Move in D Position	1	-	-	1	12.0	12.1	10-30	5-25
12.2	Force Left & Right1-5	2	-	-	1-2	12.1	12.2	5-10@	2-5@
12.21	Three Yard Lesson	2	-	-	2-3	12.2	12.21	15-30	5-15
12.22	Mirror Lesson	2	x	x	3	12.21	12.22	-	5-10
12.3	Trapping 1-3	3	-	-	2-3	12.21	12.3	15-25	10-15
12.31	Trapping Game	3	-	-	2-3	12.3	12.31	-	10-20
12.4	Front Keep Out of Lane	2	x	-	3	12.1	12.4	10-20	10-15
12.41	Front and Box Out	2	x	-	3	11.3, 12.4	12.41	10-15	10-15
12.5	Overplaying 1-6	2	x	-	1-3	10.7, 12.2	12.5	~5-30	~5-15
12.6	Defense the Low Post	2+	x	-	1-2	12.5	12.6	20-30	10-15
12.61	Low Post with Passing	2+	x	-	2-3	12.6	12.61	-	10-20
12.7	D on Shooter	2	x	x	2	5.3, 11.3	12.7	10-15	3-8
12.71	D on Driver	2	x	x	2-3	12.7, 12.21	12.71	10-20	5-10
12.72	2 on 1	3	x	x	3	12.7,9.52+	12.72	10-20	5-10
13.0	**Picking or Screening 1-2**	2+	x	x	1	10.6,10.51	**13.0**	10-15	5
13.01	Defensing the Pick	4	x	x	2	13.0	13.01	10-30	5-15
14.0	**Center Jump**	T	x	x	1-3	12.1,+	**14.0**	15-25	5-10
14.01	Practice Jumping	T	x	x	3	14.0,+	14.01	5-10	2-5
14.02	D at Center Jump	T	x	x	3	all 12,14.0,+	14.02	5-10	5
15.0	**Foul Line Transition1-3**	T	x	x	1-3	all-11,12,+	**15.0**	15-30@	10-20@
15.1	Center Jump Transition	T	x	x	1-3	14.0,15.0+	15.1	15-30	10-20
15.2	Play to Transition	T	x	x	2-3	9.6,15.0,16.0+	15.2	15-25	10-20
16.0	**Offense Setup 1-2**	T	x	x	1-2	all- 9,10,12,+	**16.0**	10-20@	5-10@
16.1	Plays 1,2,3	3	x	x	2	16.0,+	16.1	20-30	10-20
16.2	Figure 8	T	x	x	2	13.0,16.0-1,+	16.2	10-25	5-15
16.21	8 with Defense	T	x	x	2-3	all 12,16.2,+	16.21	-	10-15
17.0	**Defense-Helping Out 1-3**	T	x	x	1-3	all- 11,12,+	**17.0**	20-30	10-20
17.01	Help in Figure 8	T	x	x	1-3	17.0	17.01	-	10-20
17.1	2-1-2 Zone Shift	T	x	x	1-3	17.0,+	17.1	10-15	5
17.11	Half Court Trap Zone	T	x	x	1-3	17.1,+	17.11	10-20	5-10
18.0	**Out-of-Bounds Plays**	T	x	x	1-3	16.0,+	**18.0**	10-15	5-10
18.01	4 in Line	T	x	x	1-3	18.0,+	18.01	10-15	5-10
19.0	**Full Pressure Offense**	T	x	x	1-3	16,0,17.0,+	**19.0**	20-30	15-30
19.1	Trapping Zone Press	T	x	x	1-3	19.0,+	19.1	15-30	15-20
19.11	Switch Zone to 1-on-1	T	x	x	1-3	17.1,19.1,+	19.11	-	5-15

Chapter Six

6

Principles of Learning

•Note that the table of lessons from **The Basketball Player's Bible** follows this section, so you can better follow the lesson references in parentheses.

One big misconception about learning the basics is that to improve you must practice things millions of times. I've tried it and so has everybody else. It does not work well. Volume of practice does not necessarily bring about improvement; practicing properly insures improvement. The following **principles** tell you what and how to practice. A list of **Counterproductive Beliefs** follows. These often widely held ideas prevent learning because they do not work.

The Principles Of Shooting

1. Shooting improvement starts with technique. (1-4, 6)

2. Technique must be practiced close to the basket. (5, 7, 8, 14-23)

3. To improve your shooting range start close to the basket and gradually back off. (8 and 25)

4. To improve shooting you must shoot in a game-like situation. (9, 26-30)

5. Every shooting move, as will as every other move to dribble or to pass, starts with a pivot. So, you must be an expert at pivoting. (10-12)

Counterproductive Beliefs

1. Repetition yields improvement. This is only true to a limited degree. Improvement only follows doing things correctly. Practicing incorrectly yields problems. If you practice correctly, follow the lessons, improvement will come with much less repetition than you initially thought.

2. Only 7th graders need to practice technique. Not true. Even Hall of Famers do. Every time you play ball you need to warm up with a few minutes of shooting technique.

3. Only 7th graders need to practice close to the basket. No, everybody does for several reasons. One is that this is the best way to use and apply technique. And again I say, without technique improvement, there is no improvement. The other reason is that a great percentage of shots are taken from this area in a game. So, it is most beneficial to practice game level shooting especially in this area.

4. You can work on technique as you work on shooting. Nope. Technique and shooting need to be practiced separately. One, technique improves your shot by changing and focusing on the mechanics (movement) of the shot. You give little thought to the actual shot when working on technique. Conversely or inversely or reciprocally, thinking about technique when in the motion of shooting can only psyche you out. These two things should be practiced, and even more importantly, thought about separately.

5. If you are a good shooter in practice, then you should be a good game shooter. No. Shooting rested, under little psychological pressure or physical defensive pressure in practice is not the same as shooting under more adverse game situations. Good shooters are good game shooters.

6. You need talent to shoot well. Only naturally talented players can shoot well and learn tricky moves. Not so. Anybody can be a good shooter or dribbler, passer, etc., if they practice properly.

7. Great shooters are great players. Not so. Note that many Hall of Famers are not great shooters. Shooting is only one part of the game. If you want to be a great basketball player, you need to be as tall, strong, quick, and fast as possible. Work on being an athlete as well as practicing the skills. All Hall of Famers are great athletes.

Principles Of Dribbling

1. Dribbling starts with proper hand and arm motion as well as body position. (1, 2, 59)

2. Moving and twisting to awkward body positions are keys to dribbling. (60-62)

3. You need to dribble with defensive contact, looking in all directions, even behind, to learn how to protect the ball. (63-64)

4. Dribbling is never an end unto itself. One offensive objective is to pass the ball up court to the open player as fast as possible. You must dribble with your head up, constantly looking to pass. All lessons require players to keep their heads up and look while dribbling. (65)

Counterproductive Beliefs

1. Dribbling can't be taught. You have to be a natural.

This is true if you don't know how to teach dribbling. This inaccurate idea discourages coaches and players alike. Nothing could be further from the truth.

2. Dribbling between the legs and behind the back are effective methods. They may look good and be okay to practice, but they do not have much effect in games.

3. It is cool to dribble waist high or higher like many of the pros. Dribbling high is much more difficult, and, unless you are very quick it will lead to disaster. Bob Cousy dribbled with his elbows nearly straight; the ball was only inches, rather than feet, off the floor.

4. The more you dribble the better you dribble. No, dribbling correctly improves dribbling. Dribbling with the head down, standing straight up, not bothering to look around does the reverse–you learn how to and do dribble incorrectly. You need to be aware of how you practice. If you want to improve your dribbling technique stop dribbling improperly, even if it is inadvertent, like the dribbling you do while shooting the ball around. Limit your dribbling to the lessons in this book.

The Principles of Defense

1. You need to be in a body position than enables you to move quickly as well as maintain this position while moving. (67-68)

2. You need to stay with the offensive player. (68-77 except 75)

3. You always force the offense to one side or the other whether or not they have the ball. (69-72, 76)

4. You also must prevent low post players from moving where they want to go. It is easy to box out if you play defense properly. (72-74)

5. Defensing the pick can be tricky. It requires lots of communication and experience. (77)

6. Proper strong and weak side defense is the key to effective team defense. Weak side defenders must help out on the ball. (73-75)

7. Hustle is a big part of defense. (68-73) Hustle also includes how to catch up to an offensive player dribbling to the basket. (29)

Counterproductive Beliefs

1. Learning *on ball* defense is more important than *off ball* defense. Nope–both are of nearly equal importance. *Off ball* defense is probably more important, because four players are off the ball at any moment. One-on-one any offensive player can go around the defense. So, *off ball* players always need to help out. *Off ball* players must be in position to rebound as well.

2. Defense is difficult to learn. Nope. Defense is much easier to learn than any offensive skill. Less skill is involved. A player can become expert in weeks rather than the months or years it takes for offense.

3. You can't teach hustle. Nope. It is one of the easiest, if not the easiest, skill to teach. All of the players I ever coached hustled.

The Principles of Rebounding

1. Rebounding involves pivoting, so you need to be an expert before you start. (10-12)

2. Rebounding involves grabbing and pulling the ball away as well as pivoting. (78)

3. One key to rebounding, which is often skipped, is predicting where the ball will go. You need to watch shot arcs carefully. (79)

4. You need to be ready, in the ready position, for errant bounces and loose balls especially in a foul shooting situation. (80)

5. You need to go for offensive and defensive rebounds in a similar way. Positioning and boxing out are keys. (81, 82)

Counterproductive Beliefs

1. You need to be tall and have a 4-foot vertical jump to rebound well. Not necessarily true. These attributes help, but smarts will help just as much. Some players always seem to be around the ball even though they are short or can barely jump. These lessons make you smarter.

2. Rebounding involves just going for the ball. Not so. Good rebounders do the following things:

•Watch shot arcs and the shooter carefully and accurately predict where the ball will go.

•Step in front or get position on the opponent.

•Rarely get boxed out.

•Often come from behind the basket when needed.

The Principles of Pass Catch Cut

These skills are so interrelated that I present the principles in one section.

1. Passing technique starts with touch and wrist movement as well as arm position. Most passes involve a flick of the wrist with little arm movement. (1, 2, 34)

2. Faking is an important part of cutting technique. (52)

3. Passing as well as catching involves pivoting. (5-7, 15)

4. Use the overhead, side, and bounce pass to avoid the defense. (35-38)

5. Bounce passes, which are especially effective in traffic, need to be carefully timed. (37)

6. Baseball passes are good for long passes. (39, 40)

7. Communication is necessary to insure that the ball and the cutter meet at a point. (42)

8. Realistic passing lessons need defense. (43, 55, 56)

9. Front and back weaves are a good way to practice timing without defense in a game-like situation. (44, 45)

10. The footwork involved in catching a pass is tricky–jump, catch, step one, two. (21, 22)

11. You must catch passes before you stop running forward. (48, 49)

12. You must step in front of your opponent before going for a loose ball. (50)

13. You must attempt to catch all passes, even if the pass is off the mark. (51)

14. The key to catching passes and to team offense involves faking and cutting to the ball or open area. (47, 48)

15. The last part of a cut is a jump for the ball. Another way to say this is to always jump to the ball before you catch it. (49)

Counterproductive Beliefs

1. Good plays are the key to team offense. Nope. Players need to learn the fundamentals of offense. The greatest plays ever dreamed cannot work if players do not cut or communicate well. The worst plays ever conceived will work if players know how to cut, pass, and communicate.

2. Chest passes may have historical significance but they are worthless with defense. Holding the ball close to the body at waist height is a terrible place to have the ball. You can't pass fake, ball fake or readily reach around the offense. Neither can you fake a shot with the ball in this position. Say good-bye to this pass and use more effective ones.

3. It is easy to catch a ball. No–the footwork is quite difficult. The hands need to be in the proper position as well. I see pros and college players routinely drop passes because their hands are not clawed with fingers spread.

4. Timing between players just develops. If you can wait for evolution to take place I bet it will. However, if you practice timing it will develop within days rather than eons.

5. Passing is an easy skill. Passing as well as cutting may even be more difficult to learn than shooting or dribbling. Their are several reasons for this. One, timing between the passer and cutter is involved. Two, flicking passes is rarely taught, and it is not that easy to do. Adding defense on the passer and or catcher makes passing very difficult. Lessons 29 and 30 demonstrate just how difficult.

The Principles of Picking (Screening)

1. Picking is important when the defense is tight. Use picks either on or off the ball. (57, 58, 77)

2. Pick users rub shoulders with the pick when running by. (57)

3. Pickers remain motionless and face the cutter. (57)

4. The defense in a picking situation must communicate and coordinate the effort. (77)

Player's Table of Lessons

LESSON	NAME	ASSIST	PLAYERS	COURT	BALL	EFFORT	LESSON	Lessons Before	REF TO Coach's Manual	DAILY TIME	EXTRA
1-9	**SHOOTING TECHNIQUE**										
1	The Magic Touch	-	1	-	x	1	1	none	1.0	1-2	0
2	Flick Your Wrist	x	1	-	-	1	2	none	3.0	2	0
3	Flick Up	x	1	-	x	1	3	2	5.1	2-5	2
4	One-Inch Shot	x	1	x	x	1	4	3	5.2	5-10	1
5	One-Foot Shot	x	1	x	x	2	5	4	5.3	5-15	2
6	The No-Step Layup 1-3	x	1	x	x	1	6	1	5.4	5-20	0
7	One Step & Dribble Layup 1-3	x	1	x	x	2	7	2	5.5	5-15	1
8	Foul Shot Technique 1-3	x	1	-	x	1	8	5	5.6	2-5	2
9	Foul Shot Practice	-	1	x	x	3	9	8	5.7	5-15	0
10-12	**PIVOTING**										
10	Start Pivoting	x	1	-	-	1	10	none	2.0	5-10	0
11	Pivoting with Ball	x	1	-	x	2	11	10	2.1	2-20	0
12	Pivot with Defense	-	2	-	x	2-3	12	11	2.2	5-10	3
13-23	**MOVES**										
13	Moves-Lessons 14-23	-	x	x	x	-	13	5,11	6.0	-	0
14	Pivot Around Shoot	-	1	x	x	1-2	14	13	6.1	5-20	0
15	Pivot Backward Shoot	-	1	x	x	1-2	15	14	6.2	5-20	0
16	Step Fake Shoot	-	1	x	x	1-2	16	14	6.3	5-20	0
17	Fake Pivot Shoot	-	1	x	x	1-2	17	16	6.31	5-20	1
18	Pivot Fake Shoot	-	1	x	x	1-2	18	16	6.4	5-20	1
19	Hook Shot 1-2	x	1	x	x	1-2	19	16	6.5	5-20	0
20	Jump Hook & Fake	-	1	x	x	1-2	20	19	6.51	5-20	2
21	Step Hook & Fake	-	1	x	x	1-2	21	20	6.53	5-20	2
22	Underneath Hooks	-	1	x	x	1-2	22	21	6.55	5-20	2
23	Jump Shot	-	1	x	x	1-2	23	16	6.6	5-20	4
24-26	**PRACTICE SHOOTING**										
24	Driving to the Basket	-	1	x	x	2	24	7,16,62	8.1	5-20	2
25	Near to Far	-	1	x	x	2	25	8	8.3	5-10	0
26	Full Court Shoot	-	1	x	x	2-3	26	24,25,62	8.2	5-20	1
27-30	**PRESSURE SHOOTING**										
27	Pressure Shot	x	1	x	x	2-3	27	23	7.0	5-15	2
28	Run Stop Shoot	x	1	x	x	2-3	28	27	7.1	2-5	2
29	Catch Up	x	2	x	x	3	29	24,27	7.2	5	0
30	Defense in Face Shoot	-	2	x	x	2-3	30	5	7.3	2-5	2
31-33	**HANDLING THE BALL**										
31	Take Away	-	2	-	x	1-2	31	1	1.1	5-10	0
32	Move Ball	-	2	-	x	3	32	2	1.4	2-5	0
33	Conditioning Grab	-	2	x	x	2	33	31	1.2	15-30	2
34-45	**PASSING**										
34	Passing Technique	x	1	-	-	1	34	2,10	9.0	1-2	0
35	Overhead Short Pass	-	2	-	x	1-2	35	34	9.1	5	0
36	Side Short Pass	-	2	-	x	1-2	36	35	9.11	5	0
37	Bounce Pass	-	2	-	x	1-2	37	36	9.12	5	0
38	Back Pass	-	2	-	x	1-2	38	11,37	9.13	5	1
39	Baseball Pass	-	2	x	x	2	39	none	9.2	5	0
40	Baseball Pass Cut	-	2	x	x	2	40	39	9.3	5-10	2
41	Pivot Pass	-	2	-	x	2	41	11,36,56	9.5	5-10	1

LESSON	NAME	ASSIST	PLAYERS	COURT	BALL	EFFORT	LESSON	Lessons Before	REF TO Coach's Manual	DAILY TIME	EXTRA
42	Pass Communication 1-2	-	2	-	x	2	42	41	9.51	5	0
43	D Overhead Side Pass	-	3	-	x	2-3	43	12,42	9.6	5-10	1
44	Front Weave	-	3	x	x	2	44	37,39	9.7	10-20	0
45	Back Weave	x	3+	x	x	2	45	2,12,58	9.8	5-10	0
46-56	**CATCHING CUTTING**										
46	Catch Cut Technique	x	1	-	x	1	46	1,35	10.0	5-10	1
47	Go Fetch It	x	1	-	x	1-2	47	46	10.1	2-10	0
48	Coming to the Ball	x	1	-	x	1-2	48	47	10.11	5-10	0
49	Jump to Ball	-	2	-	x	1-2	49	48	10.2	5-10	0
50	Loose Ball Lesson	x	2	-	x	3	50	31,49	10.3	2-5	0
51	Catching Bad Passes	x	1	-	x	2	51	50	10.4	2-5	0
52	Cut Fake Technique	x	2	-	-	1-2	52	none	10.5	5-10	0
53	Cut to the Ball	-	2	-	x	2-3	53	48,52	10.6	5-15	1
54	Three Second Lesson 1-2	-	1	x	-	1	54	53	10.7	3-4	1
55	Overplay the Catcher	-	3	x	x	3	55	42,53,73	10.8	5-20	2
56	D Pass, Overplay Catcher	-	4	x	x	3	56	55	10.9	5-15	2
57-58	**PICKING (Screening)**										
57	Picking 1-2	-	2	x	-	1-2	57	none	13.0	5	0
58	Cutting off a Pick	-	3	x	-	1-2	58	57	10.51	5-15	0
59-66	**DRIBBLING**										
59	Dribbling D Position	-	1	-	x	1	59	2	4.0	1-2	0
60	Dribble Mechanics 1-2	x	1	-	x	1-2	60	59	4.1	5-15	4
61	Dribble Twist	x	1	-	x	1-2	61	60	4.13	5-15	1
62	Follow the Leader 1-3	x	1+	-	x	1-2	62	61	4.2	5-15	2
63	Protect Ball	x	2	-	x	2-3	63	62,68	4.3	5-10	2
64	Dribble with D Layup	x	1+	x	x	2-3	64	7,63	4.4	10-20	0
65	Dribble Pass with D	-	3	-	x	3	65	43,63	4.5	10-20	1
66	Dribble Full Shoot	-	1	x	x	2-3	66	7,63	8.2	5-15	0
67-77	**DEFENSE**										
67	Defensive Position	-	1	-	-	1	67	none	12.0	2-4	0
68	Move in D Position 1-3	-	1	-	-	1-3	68	67	12.1	5-25	0
69	Force Left & Right1-5	x	2	-	-	1-2	69	68	12.2	2-5@	0
70	Three Yard Lesson	x	2	-	-	2-3	70	69	12.21	5-15	1
71	Trapping 1-3	-	3	-	-	2-3	71	70	12.3	10-15	1
72	Front Keep Out of Lane	-	2	x	-	3	72	68	12.4	10-15	1
73	Overplaying 1-6	-	2	x	-	1-3	73	70	12.5	10-20@	0
74	Defense the Low Post 1-3	x	2+	x	-	1-2	74	73	12.6,17	10-15	1
75	D on Shooter	x	2	x	x	2	75	5,71	12.7	3-8	1
76	D on Driver	-	2	x	x	2-3	76	75	12.71	5-10	1
77	Defensing the Pick 1-2	x	4	x	x	2	77	58,76	13.01	10-20	0
78-82	**REBOUNDING**										
78	Rebound Grab Ball	x	1	-	x	1-2	78	1,10	11,1.4	2-5	0
79	Watching the Ball	x	1	x	x	1-2	79	none	11.1	5	0
80	Rebound Ready Position	x	1	x	x	1-2	80	79	11.11	1	1
81	Step in Front Box Out 1-2	x	2	x	x	3	81	73,80	11.2	5-10	1
82	Block Box Out 1-2	-	2	x	x	2-3	82	80	11.3	10-20	0

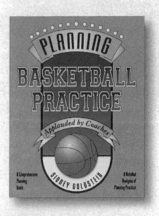

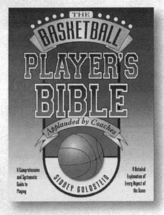

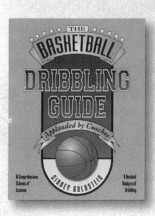
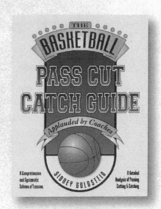
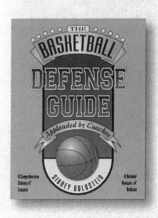

we've got videos and clinics

THE BASKETBALL COACH'S BIBLE WILL HELP YOU BY ...

✻ showing you how best to plan and run practice
✻ supplying two hundred field tested lessons ready to use
✻ systematically teaching each skill, step-by-step
✻ not skipping basic steps essential to your success
✻ presenting strategies, a warm down, game statistics and more
✻ saving you time by giving you methods and ideas that work

books

A. **The Basketball Coach's Bible**   350 pages
Everything about coaching. (07-5) $24.95

B. **The Basketball Player's Bible**   270 pages
All individual fundamentals. (13-X) $19.95

C. **The Basketball Shooting Guide** 45 pages
Yields permanent improvement. (14-8) $ 6.95

D. **The Basketball Scoring Guide**   47 pages
Teaches pro moves step-by-step. (15-6) $ 6.95

E. **The Basketball Dribbling Guide** 46 pages
Anyone can be a good dribbler. (16-4) $ 6.95

F. **The Basketball Defense Guide**   46 pages
Defense in every situation. (17-2) $ 6.95

G. **The Basketball Pass Cut Catch Guide** 47 pages
Be an effective team player. (18-0) $ 6.95

H. **Basketball Fundamentals**   46 pages
Covers all fundamentals. (08-3) $ 6.95

I. **Planning Basketball Practice**   46 pages
Use time effectively, plan, plus. (09-1) $ 6.95

J. **9 Book Series**, A - I (01-6)   ~$20 off $ 81.50 w/ship

K. **2 Book Bible Set**, A,B (20-2)   ~$5 off $ 46.13 w/ship

L. **7 Guide Set**, C - I (21-0)   ~ $5 off $ 49.50 w/ship

videos   40-60 MINUTES; $24.95 EACH
CHECK FOR AVAILABILITY

1. **Fundamentals I** Over 25 individual skill topics. (77-6)
2. **Fundamentals II** Team Skills, plays & pressure defense (90-3)
3. **Planning Practice I** Daily, weekly, and seasonal planning. (75-X)
4. **Planning Practice II** Get 5 times more out of practice. (76-8)
5. **Shooting I** Technique, Hook, Jump Shot & Layup (78-4)
6. **Shooting II** Foul Shooting, 3-Point Shooting, Driving (79-2)
7. **Shooting III** Shooting under pressure, Scoring Moves, Faking (80-6)
8. **Dribbling** Technique, Position, Protect Ball, Looking Up (81-4)
9. **Defense I** Position, Forcing, Trapping, On Shooter (84-9)
10. **Defense II** lane/Post, overplay, Front, Help, Strong-Weak (85-7)
11. **Passing I** Technique, Overhead, Bounce, Communication (82-2)
12. **Passing II** Cutting, Faking, Passing with Defense (83-0)
13. **Rebounding/Picking** Going for the Ball, Positioning, Boxing out (91-1)
14. **The Transition Game** from Foul Line, Center Jump & Plays (86-5)
15. **Team Offense** Offensive setup, Plays, Pliable Offense (87-3)
16. **Team Defense** Helping Out, Zone Shift, Half Court Trap (88-1)
17. **Full Court Pressure** Offense, Trapping Zone, Out-of-Bounds (89-X)

SIDNEY GOLDSTEIN, MR. BASKETBALL BASICS, TELLS YOU ABOUT HIS BOOKS

"This series is about fundamentals. It is a step back to the basics and a step forward to improved training methods. It is a place to start and to return again and again. No matter what your coaching level, age or sex the fundamentals do not change. You will reap great rewards by recognizing, practicing, and applying them to your situation. Visit our web site for 60 pages of information about our books, more comments from coaches, reviews, discounts, freebies, basketball articles, tips, videos, clinics, and more. I guarantee satisfaction."

clinics

VISIT OUR WEB SITE FOR DATE, TIME, AND LOCATION OF COACH AND PLAYER CLINICS:
www.mrbasketball.net

order form

QTY	ITEM	TITLE	PRICE

SHIPPING
$25 = $5; $50 = $5.75; $75 = $6.50
ADD $1 FOR HOME DELIVERY

DISCOUNTS 50-75% CALL OR CHECK www.mrbasketball.net

SUBTOTAL _____
ADD 7% SALES TAX IN PA _____
SHIPPING _____
TOTAL ORDER _____

ALL BOOKS ARE 8.5x11. ALL GUIDES COST 6.95; NEW EDITIONS COST $7.45 WHEN AVAILABLE. ALL VIDEOS COST $24.95 EACH AND RUN 45-60 MINUTES. ISBN 1-884357-(XX-X) SUFFIX IN PARENTHESIS

HOW TO ORDER
Call **1-800-979-8642**
Use our web site: **www.mrbasketball.net**
Fax PO's to: **215-438-4459**

Use your credit card, send a money order or PO to: **Golden Aura Publishing P.O. Box 41012 Phila., PA 19127-1012**

name _____
address _____
city _____ state_____ zip_____
phone _____
card #_____ exp_____ home zip_____